PENUMBRA

I0173548

An Anthology

Poets—

Quinton Hallett
Laura LeHew
Karen Locke
Nancy Carol Moody
Sharon Lask Munson
Keli Osborn
Jenny Root
Colette Tennant

Editor—

Laura LeHew

First U.S. edition 2017

Editor/Publisher: Laura LeHew

Proofreaders: Catherine McGuire
                      Roy R. Seitz
                      Harriot West

Cover: "Lopez Island Sunset"
                      © Laura LeHew, 2017

This photo snapped at dusk, the sunset with all the shadows and gradations, works as a metaphor for the underlying theme of this anthology: verge. LeHew shot this photo on Lopez Island, Washington.

Copyright © 2017   Uttered Chaos

Uttered Chaos
PO Box 50638
Eugene, OR 97405
www.utteredchaos.org

ISBN: 978-0-9889366-9-0

Laura LeHew

A NOTE OF GRATITUDE:

Thanks to the Lane Literary Guild (LLG) for its generous contribution to Uttered Chaos of $225. We extend gratitude for support of a literary work for the 1st & 3rd Thursdays critique group through its grant-making activity.

This grant was used to assist us in production of this anthology and includes works from current Lane Literary Guild/1st & 3rd Thursday members Quinton Hallett, Laura LeHew, Karen Locke, Nancy Carol Moody, Sharon Lask Munson, Keli Osborn, Jenny Root and Colette Tennant.

Grant funding is important to our literary organization and our community. This anthology showcases both the individual members and the cohesiveness of the group. We hope it will also serve as continuing outreach to the poetry community at large.

For more information on the LLG:

　　　laneliteraryguild.org

Laura LeHew

and her many hats—
Uttered Chaos Editor
Lane Literary Guild Steering Committee
1st & 3rd Thursdays Facilitator

CONTENTS

INTRODUCTION

Henry Alley, President, Lane Literary Guild, 1986, 2017

On September 28, 1986, as President of the Lane Literary Guild, I was emcee at our rather grand Writers at the Hult event in Eugene, Oregon's Soreng Theatre. It was packed because we featured an all-star cast, both regionally and internationally known. We had 500 people who had come to listen to a poet, a veteran, who would be speaking at the traveling Vietnam Memorial Wall, also three local poets, as well as Ken Kesey, with whom we had been talking and corresponding, whether directly or indirectly, for over a year. The Guild had made a huge ascent very quickly—from its founding in 1984 to being a major force in the Eugene Celebration, drawing on a sizeable grant and publishing the magazine *Pacifica* which had Lane Literary Contest finalists in it. We had started on humbler terms, collecting donations at our evenings in a Shakespeare cigar box. Now we were Hult Center material.

After the two-hour event, with the rather dramatic conclusion of Kesey's reading, I began my written epilogue, spelling out what I believed the Guild represented. A bit above myself from my pulpit in the Soreng Theatre, I affirmed that we in the Guild were "passionate believers in image, character and the sustained poetic vision of the individual—what I would call a radiant impressionism and a radiant humanism . . . . [we] are willing to take risks and gamble it all on the emotional plunge, at a time in our culture when being vulnerable is neither easy nor encouraged."

While speaking in this rather grandiloquent fashion, I was nonplussed to find the Kesey fans exiting almost row by row—definitely, for them, the final reason why they had come had been served. By the time I was done, very little of the audience remained. Now, however, thirty years later, after attending so many workshops and readings sponsored by the Guild, I still stand by what I said—although now I would choose simpler terms. We no longer have the large stage of the Writers at the Hult, but poems such as are published here still spread the word that we place image and distinction of voice above the flashy or the immediately popular. Here in this anthology we find poems that give familiar natural contexts but ask, frequently, for a symbolic interpretation, as part of what I rather lavishly called "radiant impressionism."

The Guild has covered much ground since 1986, even though we no longer have the rhetorical perch that Writers at the Hult provided. We have organized critique groups that meet regularly, have offered steering committee meetings along with open-mike and picnic opportunities; we also make available one-time workshops hosted by well-known authors. As part of years of tradition, we consistently promote our Windfall Reading Series of featured poets and writers. Thanks here are to be given to Laura LeHew for sustaining our mission of bringing the spoken word to Lane County by originating a critique group under the Guild's aegis, and for promoting the printed word in Lane County as well. Here *Penumbra* offers us works of the 1st & 3rd Thursday critique group, works which ask us to be a listener and also, at times, a deciphering oracle. What is the penumbra and what does the shape suggest to us?

The Guild invites you to experience this mystery in the tradition of "the sustained poetic vision of the individual."

BLUE MARBLE

About the trees, I could say
they were loudly red and gold
until winter descended
early that year,
her cool, slow breath snuffing
bright flames, darkening
our corner.

On the north side of this periwinkle house,
in that sharp sliver between dawn
and dusk,
I snip hydrangea
tarnished like brass,
gray-green wetness of a single bloom
shivering against the cold foundation.

Imagine a map to this town,
wending left or right, south to east,
from the Pacific, the McKenzie,
Mount Thielsen.
Use your shy hand
to draw a trail through streams
and tall trees, rocks and wind.

Diagram this place
without the interstate,
or runways stretching the edge.
Sketch an honest plan absent
the concrete ridgeline, false heat
below the surface. Name the yellow throat,
emerald fringe, genesis for water.

Keli Osborn

Can you answer the world
in real time?
Take this blue marble
into your waiting palm,
and listen:

BENIGN IS NOT ALWAYS

The second-opinion surgeon was kinder. The first cut me off, could not take his eyes off his Mickey Mouse watch. Friday afternoon golf shoe cleats flashed from a duffle by the clinic's steel door. The second surgeon kindly gave his opinion first. He never checked his watch as he considered removing a pea-size lump from its clump of worry behind my left ear. I considered the second surgeon kind to slip the "Hold Harmless" form under my pen like a love note before he split skin in a crescent to jimmy out the parotid cyst. Three decades later unremitting are the waters that diverge in that cheek. With each bite, sweet or savory, the salivary gland splits into tributaries, flowing inside my mouth and flushing down that cheek. The two surgeons are like rivers I've fished but forgot their names. I name the rivers Blame and Harmless while the other cheek fries.

( )

Her only requirements—
A garage with a shop, the blessing of crows,
Being nestled by trees.

It often came with a cresting hill,
A wallpapered darkness,
Burt and Dot.

She buried a saint under the river rocks.

DEUS EX MACHINA

It's the final act—the Dodge
a crumpled ball of blue foil and 14 years
of having-been-a-son drifting
incoherent at the wreck-strewn,
dirt-edge of brush
as the reek of train brakes dissipates.

The key cannot disengage
from this lock, and I understand
the recluse in her cave
in the thin air of the mountaintop, believing
it's possible to escape
from every last random scene.

There are so many ways of becoming blind.
In this version, a boa
cast as tumor is constricting vision
from the left and right
and just because it can't be seen
doesn't mean it isn't there.

REGRET, A CHORAL WORK

I play the music late into the night
attentive to the clear tenor voice
narrating my experience with Mother's Alzheimer's.

I weep at her loss of words
transposed in this new composition,

aware there was never the power to change,
only soften.

Orchestra leads off slowly—Andante

Solo begins   *Hangs on, hangs on, hangs on...*

Chorus merges, quickens—Accelerando
           understands in some corner
                   of her brain
                       hangs on, hangs on...

Builds to a blistering pace—Allegro   *odds and ends of life...*
                               of life...of life...piled...

Refrain repeats   *hangs on...hangs on...hangs on...*

Orchestra grows faint   *afraid she will never leave...*

Repeat   *hangs on, hangs on...*

Fades—diminuendo

I reflect on her life—
  Brooklyn tenement, three sisters, orphaned young,
  loving marriage, daughters

recollect Mother's words,
  If you live long enough you get everything.

TODAY I WILL MEMORIZE

The three words all fountains know
and the blue stripes on the boats in Levanto
and which rocks hide crawdads in the stream behind the house.
And I need to remember the story
the Atlantic tried to tell me one palm-treed night decades ago.
It wasn't sad really, although its words were heavy as salt.
If you squeeze the edges of elevator doors,
the thick rubber is fleshy as forearms.
I do remember that.

WHY SHE TOOK THE WATCH

Because a girl on the bus laughed at her red beanie.

Because she was eight, or seven, or six.

Because her teacher did not see her raised hand.

Because her little sister broke the doll.

Because the bed was too small for three kids.

Because she wanted something of her own.

Because there were too many rows of daffodils to weed.

Because her mother did not hear.

Because she forgot her father's hard hand.

Because the watch was bright, sparkly gold.

Jenny Root

A BETTER CALENDAR

March
arrow green shoot, new flame
augur Equinox of dark and light
birth scattered by squirrels
branches red with buds

April
chlorophyll rises, compost cooks
cut daffodils in every room, cut tulips
dawn an earlier pleasure
day stays out past curfew

May
endive and escarole
enter heat and her retinue of flies
fancy the lilacs' scented bordello
fingerling potatoes pulse underground

June
given sun and sun: abundance
green saturation calling her name
heartstop tomatoes an heirloom promise
hours of day yield minutes to night

July
ice cream, iced coffee, ice tea
irrigation early and late
jiving the honey bees' hive
June sings June, sings July

August
knotweed feathers the stillness
knotweed invasion on the rise
listen to cicadas' jazz, lovers,
listen, sweat cooling scented skin

September
marriage of tomatoes, mozzarella & basil
marriage of morning chill, fleece & flannel
night takes day's hand walking a dusty path
now the harvest, now the turning leaves

October
oak fires in the hearth stove
orchestral sunsets, strings of salmon, coral & gold
patterns of geese language writ in grey sky
patterns of orange boletes

November
quell the silent sadness
quiet the somnolent fog
remember me, morning, lost in night's embrace
remember me, dead ones, returning through the veil

December
seed catalogs on the nightstand, gathering dreams
seed potatoes in the cellar, growing eyes
telling, the seal dreams of polar bears
trumpet, the peal of first light across the ice

Jenny Root

January
under the rain, light ushers the day
under the soil, warming rooms of worms
verdant a promise, a secret to be revealed
vital the long sweet kiss of rain

February
weather a symphony, whether the sun
wherever a pea, a calendar begun
x-ing through the mulch of old leaves
xanthophyll rises within the green

March
year out, year in
yellow slickers in the mist
zed signals an ending
zenith the heavens above

TO THE HUNTER, BECAUSE OF A RED FOX AT DUSK
a tritina

If you can, consider certain prey off limits. Like the red fox
whose pungent lair rarely comes to light,
whose fur copes with your stealth, with open season craze.

Running or standing still on snow that's crazed
with star drip and bough swipe, like you this fox
hunts what moves, what holds the last breath's light.

If you sense a dash at the speed of light
and think you know how she will move, do not be crazed.
Put down your gun. Substitute another meme for fox.

Spare her from being the last wild fox. Divert the beam of your crazy
cocked light.

A FOREST ARGUMENT LEADS TO SEA

Boots seeking traction on moss-slicked stones
don't heave themselves one in front of the other
because they're looking forward
to the going-back—

such meticulous muscling up the forest path
presupposes a terminus. No, that's not right—
a fulcrum's more like it, a place to balance
before deciding where next to head.

Eventually the firs in their scraggy coats
start looking like surrender. A significant portion
of ambient roar is no longer attributable
to held breath letting loose through tree tops.

Whisked-aside ferns grow crisp around the edges;
thermals crisscrossing dank humidity
give way to sting and face-slap—
that's salt air scouring the headlands!

And then this—blue running headlong into more blue.
A wild strawberry surprises
with its almost-painful pucker of red,
green flat fans of leaves runnel down basalt castoffs

flanking the dry crumble underfoot.
What leads to the brink has been ground down.
Here, at the limit, when boot-toe strikes surface
there remain just two possible outcomes: kick of sand

spuming a parody of sea spray, or hard slam
into cliff-wall, geologic equivalent of the glottal stop.
But isn't this what we've wanted all along—to have it
one way or the other, nothing in-between?

HEDGE-RIDER

To be given away at birth
is to be buried at the crossroads.
The shining part of you moves on to be
loved by angels holding sweet milk and roses.
Those who buried you work to forget
your small, anonymous bones
hidden in the dust. Though their feet walk
back and forth across the place where you lie,
their priestly duties are stern.

No more sharing body and blood.
When the heavy bell groans,
they shut the book of family names,
dash to the ground
their sheep-tallow candles.

Part of you lies there, silent,
where birds don't sing and dogs don't bark.
The crossroads—swept clean at midnight
every full moon—they lead, as Oedipus hoped,
anywhere but home.

RUSH HOUR

Five twenty-five in the parking garage, late
September, sun too bright for tired eyes.
I climb, others race, gym shoes thrumming,
stairwell humming this last day of work
before tomorrow.

Third floor landing I stop to breathe,
what a week, and stare: Is that a cat? Black
silhouette atop the building across the street?
Faces the sun. Doesn't move.
Why is she there?

Gym shoes thrumming up and down the stairs.
Rattle of keys, laughter somewhere.

REVEALED

I thought he must be her third or fourth. One never asks. A whirlwind romance she had told me. When I met her new husband I was dumbstruck, gazed upon a Cary Grant look-alike: tall, thin, an imposing man. His dark hair lay neatly parted. His blue-striped shirt starched, collar, button-down. He took my hand with an old-fashioned demeanor. His roguish smile was like riots of color in an untamed garden.

> hot breezes
> in the sultry air
>
> s
> c
> e
> n
> t
> of sweet peas

I see her alone—in theaters, restaurants, about town. Her wide brimmed hat eclipses a solitary figure. She tells me he has his own ways. A lifetime of habits! Stays in at night. Goes to bed early. Doesn't try new foods. Won't sample curry, cumin, or cardamom. Doesn't care for garden fresh or green. Every night he makes his own dinner: ham and cheese on white bread, dab of yellow mustard, chips, canned soup. He eats in front of the television, watching football. In other seasons he varies the sports: basketball, baseball, golf. She eats alone at the kitchen table turning pages.

> breath catching cold
> f
> o
> g
> on the valley floor
> hoarfrost on fence posts

EXTINCTION

Complaining of leaves, neighbors
last week cut down three maples,
sawed off every limb. Branches
fill their yard, inviting squirrels

going nowhere. Above my house,
crows chatter for hours. Do they
know of the Hawaiian cousin,
oblivious to possible mates, semen

coaxed by human hand for feathered
offspring? When great elephants fall
to poachers on the East African savanna,
does the earth tremble? Shallow graves

scar the ground where gentle tusks lift
the dead, survivors grieve motionless kin.
Snowdrop, rosewood, Wollemi pine:
disappearing. We are the asteroid this time.

The final wave of bright yellow frogs
lives in a zoo, cast from Eden, a cloud
forest. Windows at another latitude fasten
against thickening air, machinery purr.

A man presses a child to the ground,
and I look again—just lovers in the grass,
ensnared. Sticky fruit and heat splay across
the afternoon. Even the kitchen floor is a trap.

SALT

soaking in a tub braided with lemon verbena arnica
bath salts—a storm rolls in crashes
into the ocean a gust ambers a seagull
freezes it in time

my toothbrush has broken you
are asleep some other where
a pillar of the community an
old wound scabbing over

arnica in a cut causes scarring

twelve year olds purchase
White Lightning and Hurricane Charlie
bath salts laced
with mephedrone and
methylenedioxypyrovalerone
hallucinogens
snorted, smoked, or just plain
shot-up

get out their knives, slit their throats, bellies, random
body parts
in the end they
retrieve their parents' guns
barrels on tongues pull
the triggers

salt dries the cells until they are dead

I smacked my knee on the nightstand the
place between

soft puffy skin and the bone
leaving
an abrasion

Karen Locke

LEARNING TO LOVE DANDELIONS

Season after season they bogart the grass, I want to obliterate
them, shoo them away like pesky flies, trap them like field mice,
stomp them flat as boards. Ben the horticulturist declares
they're inevitable, will always be with us, like fleas, mosquitoes.
You must learn to love them as you love bees.

I work at it, consider dandelion virtues: liver tonic,
one of nature's great medicines, plus salad greens, even wine.
I picture children blowing the fluffy seeds, fairies granting wishes.
Okay, I'll accept a few here and there, but I'll dig
others until my fingers stiffen to tough roots.

This early spring, dandelions swarm like countless yellow insects,
later a milky way of white feathery heads bursts, scatters
soft stars across the sky. The mass of stems teems with a life
of its own. But wait! Look there and there! Goldfinches, sparrows
forage and feast in blessed dandelion chaos.

MISSIVE

There's a letter in the mail that didn't mean
what it said
when it left the house.

Carrier pigeon tangled
in the ribbon of no-turning-back.

Snapping turtle in the postman's tray

riding in on a stamp
with a flag named *Forever*.

The little toy truck toddles down the lane
on the right side
of the cinematographer's split screen

carrying its happy load
of wishbooks and baked cookies.

Musical notes twirl in the trees.

And now from the left
the camera zooms in on that single envelope,

black script darkening
as it edges
near delivery.

Too late, screech the wheels.
Too late, slams the mailbox lid.

Is it any wonder
I keep looping

through this video of the sinkhole,

the acres of cypress towering one instant
on the brink
and then in the next

vanished into the abyss.

CENTRIFUGAL FORCE

Like a bat, you cling with others to the wall of a barrel,
headhandsbackheels pressed against its sides.

Moments ago you stood
on the solid platform grounded

by this excursion to the county fair
but not yet by what it portends.

Too frightened by other rides, the Bullet
or the seasick Ferris Wheel,

you chose the barrel's tall walls
and gradual tilt from horizontal to vertical.

You did not—do not to this day—
know how you can think yourself securely anchored in time

then have everything you knew about gravity
vanish in seconds.

Who hears your shrieks
left back there in frozen hover?

SHE WOKE TO THE SOUND OF HER OWN LAUGHTER

and in that moment, *if* she had woken him, to speak of her dream, she could have carried the vision all day: the train to Istanbul, the dining car, polished wood, starched linen, heft of crystal, the sleek Gatsby dress on her back—chocolate silk, onyx beading.

If she carried the dream all day, she could have tried on different beginnings, endings: the Turkish Sultan, the charade, murder, double-deal trickery, perhaps an escape through the old walled city—uncertainty that made the danger so thrilling. She could have lived a fable or an epic poem.

But as she lay there with laughter on her lips, she nodded off, and on wakening, the dream was gone, her mouth dry.

>   angle of moonlight
>   parted curtains

Jenny Root

FIRST DAFFODIL

First daffodil of the year—
so small, so diminutive

it takes ten more minutes
of my morning routine—

fixing lunch, packing files—
and then the sight

of a slight yellow slicker
on a child in the mist

to help me
remember.

Keli Osborn

ANOTHER NEW YEAR'S DAY

She thinks about the oyster grey fog
swallowing sunlight, golden orb burrowed
deep into a slit in the sky like an irritant.
She thinks about ocean time, the sad swarm
of sea life drowning in hot brine.

She considers the man who stumbled
from his truck, stabbed by the wrong knife
given to his girlfriend for Christmas,
about news of another woman crushed
between halves of a bridge, boat passing below.

She contemplates the promises of others
to dance more, breathe deeply—weighs
outrage, the case for encrypted data,
inflammatory fats. She ponders a mouse
on the back patio, nosing for seed tossed

when winter snowfall stranded tiny birds.
She thinks about toothpaste on the counter,
missing Sunday papers, cold bedroom floor,
about the fence sagging toward collapse
atop roses or the neighbor's random grandson.

She thinks about resolutions, mere letters
from revolutions, about the hope and pain
propelling pilgrims across waters and borders.
She reflects on the push and pull of change,
what must be required for transformation.

She smiles as she turns over last night's book
in her mind, author conceding *Busy* as the new

default, everyone essential, rushing, stuffing.
How are you? deserves a different answer: *I'm hot,*
I've got a tune stuck in my head, I want a cup of coffee.

She bundles for a walk, ambles by a scarlet dragon
defending empty garden beds and nearby
withered plants. She watches a young man vacuum
his car, the whir a winter mosquito piercing the air.
She passes a long man with orange hair mussed

from last night's revelry, his stovepipe legs wrapped
in denim, black suit jacket three sizes too tight.
She imagines heads rattling inside football helmets
when men crash into one another, mulls Vitamin E
and crossword puzzles as antidotes to dementia.

She recalls the way her son and teammates embraced
like bear cubs at wrestling matches, hears the rhetoric
of a new year: fresh beginnings, peace, prosperity.
She moves the clean, wet dishrags from washer
to dryer—presses the button labeled "Start."

Laura LeHew

SOME ASSEMBLY MAY BE REQUIRED

you are in denial
your eyes are hyacinth red
you page through your daughter's wedding album
you flood 1,000 lakes with tears
you lie
& you say it's about her
divorce
you buy a kayak
you buy an oar but
not a lifejacket not a helmet
ask *who wants to look through this with me*
one more time you fear
you might have missed something
you could have missed anything
you lost your house after your heart
attack
but now
submerged you ask & you ask & you ask
why not you
& already there is so much water
in the binder the hospital gave you to navigate around
your husband &
you get a purple *caregiver* ribbon—pin it on your long sleeve
shirt you are so cold—your
friends all come to visit you crash into end-stage
you become proficient at chemo-day valet parking
at first you thought you would be the one to go
you confess your grief
you dry your eyes
hop up to make lasagna
his favorite
your husband suddenly has been diagnosed—

Laura LeHew

esophageal cancer and you
you wish you could remember if
you could swim

OCTOBER AGAIN

Early October, it begins. Down the round brown hills
of Paso Robles, off balmy beaches at Santa Cruz, out of San Francisco
fog, over Mendocino hills and Sonoma vineyards, ghosts
trudge up the coast to this green valley where fir boughs fly
in gusty wind and slant rain.

Ghosts glide by: mother, sisters, husbands, friend after friend,
too many to count this cruel October, and here comes death
like the year before and the year before that, toehold in the door
all month and into November. So what do you want to know,
Mr. Death? Whether I still believe in something?

People exist and then they do not. This day yellow and brown leaves rattle
to the hard ground: no crimson, bronze, gold to behold. A red
button mushroom sprouts from a small hollow in the vine maple.
Warblers return to harvest insects from gray lichen.
This night a lunar eclipse.

PENUMBRA
after Mark Strand

Open the book of midnight
to the page where the attic appears

somewhere between the rib cage
and the empty hand

next to the tree you always
wanted to name Nicodemus—

there where the white swan floats
across the water like a lazy angel,

where everything waits by the edge
of the Hunter's moon,

wanting to be read and reread—
to be tasted by your quiet tongue.

ACKNOWLEDGMENTS & NOTES

Thanks to the editors of the following journals and books in which these poems first appeared, sometimes in altered versions or with different titles:

LeHew, Laura. "(   )" is in the form of a Sevenling.

LeHew, Laura. "Salt." 2nd Place in the Anything Goes Contest 2012 from Wild Age Press and was published as a broadside that accompanied a bottle of bath salts. 2014.

LeHew, Laura. "Some Assembly May Be Required." *The FemLit Magazine.* 2016.

Moody, Nancy Carol. "A Forest Argument Leads to Sea." *The House of Nobody Home*, FutureCycle Press. 2016.

Moody, Nancy Carol. "Missive." *The House of Nobody Home*, FutureCycle Press. 2016.

Munson, Sharon Lask. "She Woke to the Sound of Her Own Laughter." *Braiding Lives*, Poetica Publishing. 2014.

Osborn, Keli. "Blue Marble" was the winner in the Write to Publish 2016 Pacific Northwest Poetry Contest, presented by Ooligan Press and *The Timberline Review*, and was published by *The Timberline Review* in its Winter/Spring 2016 volume.

Osborn, Keli "Extinction." *Elohi Gadugi Journal*, Winter 2016: The Coming Storm. 2016.

Osborn, Keli. The book reference for "Another New Year's Day" is *Encyclopedia of an Ordinary Life*, by the late Amy Krouse Rosenthal, who died in March 2017. [New York: Three Rivers Press. 2005.]

Root, Jenny. "First Daffodil." *Thresholds Literary Journal*, Unitarian Universalist Church of Eugene. Spring 2009.

Root, Jenny. "A Better Calendar." *Elohi Gadugi Journal*, Spring/Summer 2013, and in *Narratives for a New World*, Vol, 1 2012–2013 anthology, Elohi Gadugi Books, 2013.

Tennant, Colette. "Hedge-Rider." *Commotion of Wings*, Main Street Rag. 2010.

BIOGRAPHIES

Quinton Hallett writes and edits from her rural property in Noti, Oregon. She is the author of three chapbooks, founder of Fern Rock Falls Press, and her work appears or is forthcoming in journals and anthologies including: *Windfall*, *Ayris*, *Tiger's Eye*, *Paper Nautilus*, *CIRQUE*, *The Knotted Bond*, *Till the Tide*, and *december*. She has coordinated a reading series and high school poet visits for the Oregon Poetry Association, and received residencies from Caldera and Soapstone. She reads a selection of poems on the Oregon Poetic Voices website (oregonpoeticvoices.org). In 2013, an animated short film by John Haugse featured one of her poems, "To the Long Ago Maybes." In a previous incarnation, Quinton organized exhibitions for the Smithsonian Institution Traveling Exhibition Service (SITES) and the Armand Hammer Foundation in Los Angeles.

Laura **LeHew** lives in the realm of possibility, where anything can happen. She is constantly thinking of new ideas and themes to convey in her work. Her intent is to create works that are formally and aesthetically engaging while conceptually connecting with the everyday: to reify the ordinary into the extraordinary, to question realities—social, political and otherwise. Poetry is a way to explore and understand those ideas which frustrate and confront her.

Widely published, Laura's collections include: *Becoming* (Another New Calligraphy) a non-linear discourse on alcoholism and dementia, *Buyer's Remorse* (Tiger's Eye Press, Infinities Collections—forthcoming), *Willingly Would I Burn,* (MoonPath Press) themed around math and science, *It's Always Night, It Always Rains,* (Winterhawk Press) noir and *Beauty* (Tiger's Eye Press) fairy tales. Laura received her MFA from CCA. She owns and edits Uttered Chaos, a small press which publishes books of poetry. Laura knows nothing of gardens or gardening but is well-versed in the cultivation of cats.

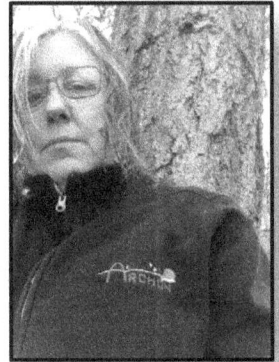

utteredchaos.org ● lauralehew.com

The following publications have included poems by Karen Locke: *Calyx, 13th Moon, Luckiamute Four, Alaska Quarterly Review, The Eugene Anthology of Writers #1* (Northwest Review Books), *Ploughshares, Fireweed, The Absence of Something Specified* and others. After a long hiatus devoted to teaching and family, she is writing poetry again and is honored to be included in the 1st & 3rd Thursday Poetry Group.

Karen Locke: I imagine my writing process is similar to that of many others. I keep extensive notebooks filled with ideas: something someone said, something I read, a news item, a quotation, an encounter, the view outside the kitchen window, a dream, word lists, images. I try to keep regular writing times throughout the week. Once I have a draft of a poem, I revise and revise some more, keeping in mind a quotation attributed to Charles Dickens: "Writers don't write, they rewrite."

Sometimes I write from prompts provided in Toni Hanner's Jump Start group, a place to explore and experiment with ideas and forms. Some poems simply arrive almost complete. Others take years to finally evolve to a place that feels finished enough for now. It's not uncommon for a poem to change substantially after some years have passed. A poem that took years to feel ready for an audience is "Learning to Love Dandelions" in this anthology. I had complained to the young man working in my yard about the multitude of dandelions taking over. His philosophy was not to fight them but to accept some of them. "You must learn to love dandelions," he wisely stated.

Soon after, thinking of a poem, I listed what I knew about dandelion virtues. Several years later, I wrote eight short lines containing details a poem might reveal. Even later, I saw goldfinches feeding on dandelion seeds; that experience gave me a way to both end the poem and to see how the tone and images in the poem could connect. At least four drafts after that, I took the poem to the 1st & 3rd Thursday Poetry Group where seven smart, talented, generous, and good-humored women gave excellent advice, some of which I incorporated into the version in this anthology.

Nancy Carol Moody: I don't think of myself as writing poems so much as constructing them, each one an assemblage of images and random thoughts ultimately strung together in (what I hope is) a cohesive arrangement. This method complements my parallel life as a maker of collages; happiness is holding a pen or a pair of scissors in my hand. I am the author of two collections, *The House of Nobody Home* and *Photograph with Girls* as well as the 8-poem chapbook, *Mermaid*. When I'm not on a train, I live in Eugene, Oregon.

http://nancycarolmoody.com

Different things motivate me to write. A mood. A memory. The smell of cooking. Burning leaves. A windy day. Rain. Fog. Music. Someone or something I observe or overhear—and, of course, imagination. I have a pin that says, "I Make Things Up." It's important for me to have my own office. I took over a spare bedroom, emptied it of bed and dresser and moved in the essentials: a desk for my computer, a bookshelf, a file cabinet, and an old cushioned chair of my mother's that goes back to my childhood. From my upstairs office window, I look out on tall oaks. The trees and the changing seasons add a kind of peace that makes writing possible.

Sharon **Lask Munson** was born and raised in Detroit, Michigan. She taught in England, Germany, Okinawa and Puerto Rico before driving to Anchorage, Alaska and staying put for the next twenty years. She is a poet, retired teacher, coffee addict, wine lover, old movie enthusiast— with many published poems, two chapbooks, and one full-length book of poetry. She now lives and writes in Eugene, Oregon.

www.sharonlaskmunson.com

Keli Osborn: My lapel button says "Ink is my perfume." I love language: sounds of letters and words, differing looks text can take. I write for pleasure, to seek meaning and connect with others, to open a door. I live with family in Eugene, Oregon, where I work with community arts, environmental and civic organizations. My poems have appeared in *San Pedro River Review*, *The Quotable* and *Delaware Poetry Review*, as well as in several anthologies including *All We Can Hold* and *The Absence of Something Specified*.

J
enny Root's work has appeared in many literary journals including *basalt*, *Crab Creek Review*, *Cloudbank*, *Elohi Gadugi Journal*, *Windfall* and *CIRQUE* and anthologized in *What the River Brings: Oregon River Poems* and *New Poets of the American West*. Her first collection, *The Company of Sharks* was published by Fae Press in 2013. A two-time fellow at PLAYA Artists & Writers Residency in southern Oregon, she works as an editor and event planner for an educational nonprofit in the field of criminal justice based in Eugene, Oregon.

Colette **Tennant**'s first book of poetry, *Commotion of Wings*, was published by Main Street Rag in 2010 as an Editor's Choice. Her poetry was nominated for a Pushcart Prize in 2014. Her second poetry book, *Eden and After*, was published by Tebot Bach July, 2015. She has had poems published in various journals, including *Southern Poetry Review*, *The Dos Passos Review*, and the *Prairie Schooner*. She lives in Salem, Oregon. This is her twenty-third year as an English Professor at Corban University where she teaches poetry writing, creative writing, and many literature classes.

ABOUT 1ˢᵗ & 3ʳᵈ

Poetry is not only dream and vision; it is the skeleton architecture of our lives. It lays the foundations for a future of change, a bridge across our fears of what has never been before. ~Audre Lorde

The day after graduating with my MFA in Poetry from the California College of Arts I decided to move from San Francisco to Eugene, Oregon. I had just joined Kim Addonizio's private critique group. It was fabulous. I didn't want to give it up. The only people I knew in Eugene were my now ex-husband and the contractors working on the house. Kim suggested I contact Dorianne Laux. Dorianne and Joe were just moving to North Carolina and suggested I contact the Lane Literary Guild.

The Guild pointed me to Gary Adams who had room in his group *P3*. I was in that group for a while when Robin Saxton was asked to form the next group for the Guild. She did and I moved into her group, *P4* otherwise known as *Poetry4*. And then, I took it over. Eventually. There was no coup. She was spending more time painting. It was a natural transition. Somewhere in there I became a member of the Guild's steering committee, where I remain to this day.

I changed the name from *P4* to the *Let Them Eat Cake Poets*. We had cakes at every birthday. There were, it seemed, a lot of birthdays. After enough turnover and after we gave up cake, the group eventually re-named itself the *Rhetorical Devices*, the RDs for short.

After Rhetorical Devices grew too large, we split the group somewhat in half and formed 1ˢᵗ & 3ʳᵈ Thursday poets. Some poets moved to 1ˢᵗ & 3ʳᵈ, some stayed in Rhetorical Devices, some joined both groups. There was a lot of discussion. After a short amount of time, Colette Jonopulos said she was interested in taking the group over and that seemed like a great idea. Sadly, Colette moved to Colorado but then, happily, Nancy Carol Moody took over facilitation of the group. Several years later 1ˢᵗ & 3ʳᵈ Thursdays came back to me to facilitate.

Laura LeHew

We have had a lot of successes: poems published, books published, nominations and awards. We owe it all to the commitment of each of our members to honor and respect all the individual members, showing up week after week, doing the work (writing, reading, going to readings, etc.) and by encouraging our members to write in their own voices. It has been a pleasure to facilitate this amazing group.

Laura LeHew

www.ingramcontent.com/pod-product-compliance
Lightning Source LLC
Chambersburg PA
CBHW032058040426
42449CB00007B/1130